Freedom, Justice & Equality

Khalil Ali

King and Queen Publishing, LLC

All Rights Reserved. No part of this publication may be used either in print or electronic form without the written consent of King and Queen Publishing, LLC. Published in the United States by King and Queen Publishing, LLC.

Copyright © 2016 by Khalil Ali

Cover illustration by Khalil Ali

ISBN 978-0-9974226-1-0

For more information regarding personal appearances, interviews or purchases please contact the publisher at:

King and Queen Publishing, LLC

www.kingandqueenpublish.com
contact@kingandqueenpublish.com

This book is dedicated to all those that have lost their lives either to the casket or to the penial system due to the injustice and lack of knowledge. I pray that each and every one of you were able to find peace.

Table of Contents

Open Letter 1
Liberty or Death 3
I Don't Know 5
Sit and Wonder 7
Could Be Me 8
The Letter 9
Broke Life 11
Tomorrow and Today 12
Is it Me 14
Fight On 16
Meaningful/ Meaningless 18
Good Times 19
Soul of the Stars 21
Dear White America 23
Pretend ish Talking 28
The American Dream 30
Conversation 32
What Do You See 37
Silence 39
Final Goal 41
Individual 43
Racing Race 45
Souls of Black Folks 47
Justice or Else 49

Blind Men	52
Consciously Stupid	54
Beaten Heart	56
MLK	58
Heaven or Hell	59
Double Talk	61
Fred Hampton	62
Pawn Stars	64
Word Usage	66
Thoughts on America	70
Complaining About A Complaint	71
The Sisters	73

Open Letter

My dear brothers and sisters; I am at a loss for words at the moment, so if I begin to speak out of line please forgive me. I am not sure as to these replies (whether they are concerning what I said last week or not) therefore, I shall be as open as possible. I am not now nor at any time a scenic nor or person that believes that the "glass is half empty", I am however a realist and as a realist I believe that now is the time for us as a people, a nation, an ummah of ONE to rise from our sleep and begin to hold ourselves accountable for what is taking place in the world today. How many of us have witnessed a monstrosity taking place and simply taken the weakest form of disapproval of it? --i.e. in our heart. We must begin to now take action against all those things that we know are wrong and detrimental to not only our well being but also the well being of our children, neighbors, country men, and our kinsman afar.

There are so many of our young brothers and sisters that are dying mentally and spiritually, (not just physically) yet we continue to sit back and do nothing. When we don't begin to change it ourselves how can we possibly expect Allah to change it for us? We as descendants of Adam should begin to behave as OUR brother's keeper and not as strangers in the woods. Last jumuah I was so fortunate to be able to speak on being human and what it really means; the word itself has been completely understated and over looked for far too long. The word human comes from the Latin word *Humanus* which means Earth, which in Hebrew *Adam* means Human, which refers to *Adamah* meaning Ground. Are you beginning to see the connection? We are from "Adam", in which he was form from the "ground", his name means ground and the man, part of human, means a creature of responsibility. Ergo we are a dirt creature of responsibility and there is only ONE Earth, which has many colors to its dirt. We are one nation that has many colors to our people yet we are still only one. It was through the passage of time that we began to disperse and create differentiating characteristics between us. I am not going too in depth at the moment but I needed to get your minds to thinking of something else besides what you see and picture what you don't see. We still carry the one thing that unites us all, not just the spirit of Allah but the one thing that was imprinted within us to study and learn from- an atom. I shall leave you with that for now. Inshallah we shall communicate more later…

Fimanallah
(In the protection of Allah)

Liberty or Death

History tells us that we are a product of what we feed our minds

Failure and mistakes were made by those who didn't heed the lessons of the times

Our ancestors would disown and curse us if they knew what we were up to

After all look at all the beatings, lives lost, dog and hose fights they had to go through

It's no surprise that by closed eyes we've become lost due to our own lack of knowledge

Day after day and year after year we are becoming more and more like a tree losing its foliage

We lost our respect, pride, dignity and dreams of hope for tomorrow

Slowly we continue to kill ourselves and take our flesh and bones to the marrow

Why must we continue to travel the path of destruction and death?

When all the long there's been a better path of success and immense wealth

So give me liberty, to hell with death!

I Don't Know

How many of us have heard a child say that they "don't know" why they did something that they shouldn't have? The response is normally "why don't you know" and for some reason we think that this young person, this child does when in fact they don't and couldn't. Seriously people how could they when most adults don't know themselves. Think of the last few times you did something then not long after thought- "why did I do that?" The truth is our reason developed from the child yet it's still the same, simply put curiosity and the flesh is weak although the spirit is willing. How could we possibly be in a state of amazement by their response when in fact it is the basic root to all of our responses, regardless of how we may twist it? Once we begin to really evaluate our thoughts and actions before we actually carry them out we could begin to find ourselves with a lot less mistakes in our past, regret in our mind and an extremely sufficient amount of time not wasted. Don't get me wrong, we will not avoid all mistakes because some mistakes are so far down the line that our ability to foresee them may be limited however, through development even those may eventually be avoided as well. Imagine that, a perfect world…WOW! I don't think so; not going to happen; there isn't any balance in that world. We make these mistakes not simply because "we're human" but because through these mistakes we gain knowledge of self and life.

Once we begin to understand exactly what it is we have learned/ supposed to learn we begin to acquire wisdom which is applied knowledge. This is why wisdom comes with age so the phrase "keep on living" is true; the longer we live, the more we experience, the more we learn, the more we grow, hence the better we are able to direct others.

Sit and Wonder

Why must I sit and wonder as what is to come
Day in and day out I sit and wonder of where I come from
I think on future time and where I shall be
How, when, and why the path I travel shall take me
Walk steadily and persistent on my journey to a time unbeknown
Deep contemplation of past mistakes and hopes becoming fully grown
I wonder where shall I be in life and at point will it all make sense
Sometimes I still feel like that 10 year old climbing that 8ft fence
They say life's a B so death must be a Saint
Because all I hear now is couldn't and wouldn't, so upon my death I shouldn't hear can't
All this negativity that's being poison to my very being
Move over clouds for my ray of sunshine, because seeing is believing.

Could Be Me

That could be me with the 2012 new high dollar car
That could be me in the multilevel house that can only be seen from afar
That could be me strolling through the park with wife and children in accompaniment
That could be me with everything going smooth and having nothing to vent
But life is more than me and my vein desires
Taking nothing with me when my time has expired
Storing up warehouses of everlasting material that's destined to ease my transition
Ideological mishaps of confusion that encroach upon perdition
Purgatory calling my name towards it with thoughts of advancement
Take care and head the signs of the changes that are upon you
Move swiftly and silently as the enemy is very near and true
Stop, look and listen to that which is above all that which was created
Life is more than what you perceive, life is what you choose to make it.

The Letter

October 24, 2007

Dear Kendell,

    Hello my brother, I know that we haven't always seen eye to eye but I just want you to know that I love you regardless. I know that my time has come to an end and that it's time that you regain complete control but I just thought that I would impart a few thoughts unto you before I relinquish my position. The first being I hated those days when we fought especially since I knew you only tried to help, I only wish that you had more faith in me and perhaps I in you. Second, please take good care of our home, more so than you did last time because that mess has yet to be fully cleaned up. Third, you cannot stay as long as you did before; you turned what was supposed to be a short vacation into a long moving in process. Please do a good job in protecting our home from being vandalized or worse. I'm trusting you my brother to guard things while I'm away, although I'm not sure as to how long.

Sometimes I feel like maybe there's enough room for the both of us in here but just as soon as a major disagreement occurs, I quickly realize that there isn't. I believe that if it was completely up to you, I wouldn't be here, that you would just do as you please; not so much as caring what happened around you just as long as you got your way. I had hoped that my compassion, love, respect and honor would eventually rub off onto you but I guess not. So in a sense, I am your counterpart to keep the balance between good (me) and evil (you). Truth be told, I am not ready to have you come back like that. You may visit on an as needed basis but to move back in is not what is desired. So what I guess I'm saying is- I'm not leaving just yet, I think I shall continue to stay; I like it here and so does everyone else. So just know that although you may show your face, I have too many people depending on me to stay put so put I shall stay. I do wish you well and if I need to, I mean really need to; I know how to reach you.

Take care my brother.

Sincerely,

Khalil

Broke Life

There is nothing more humbling than being broke

No money in the pocket and the bank is the Bank of Joke

However, life is much simpler when you don't have to worry about being robbed

Practice on me… forget that mess I'll still turn you into a shish kabob

I may not have anything for you to take from me

But you do and I need big time money

Empty your pockets and give up your loot

Make it quick, fast and in a hurry before you get my size 12 boot

Stick your hands up sucka!! So how do you like it now??

Tomorrow and Today

If tomorrow never came and today was never here

What could have ever been the real fear?

For in that thought yesterday never was so tomorrow couldn't be

Thoughtless words, senseless emotions and misplaced acts that cease to surprise me

The sun won't glow and the moon refuses to shine

Water burning my soul so heat can cool my mind

Foot prints on the clouds while scattered sand rains all around

Time that no longer matters because space can no longer be found

Today we sleep; another nightmare in loom

Yesterday's slumber forgot the ultimate dream of gloom

Forget about memories as those memories escape the thoughts of days

Sleep today and tomorrow for 40 nights and 40 days

Tell no one of everything so everyone will always know

Of cloudless rain bringing the harsh summer snow

Regardless of how many imaginable fathoms of uncanny witty nature may appear

Tomorrow never came and today was never here.

Is it Me

Is it me and my thinking that has brought me here?

Or was it the actions that transpired that caused this long drawn out tear

A drop in the bucket for karma because for me it has come to be

Please God forgive me for the sorrow that I gave to she

Was it my venomous talks, depressive thoughts or just my devilish grin?

A mixture of each perhaps that caused misery to set right on in

It's funny but not so humorous how one boy could affect so many

How he could bring about Bill Gates to wake up without one copper penny

So who is to blame, I do seriously believe it has got to be him

Him being the Evil that caused a rift and time lost between them

One thing that's for sure true love can never be forgotten or lost

It will one day find its way back together again regardless of the eminent cost

So the question of will the two ever become one again

Will no longer be a question of "is it me" but rather a statement of, it's not because of me that it had to end.

Fight On

It's time again for another winter's frost

Season has come and gone yet time still is lost

Another hour slipped by without so much as a moment to see

Invisible son of the invisible man lies he

Laying there still here but travelling elsewhere

Mentally battling a war of a good and evil spiritual affair

So many against a vast many but it only takes one to win it all

To lose it all can also be done by one although it comes with a hard fall

Winter freezes again so that spring can provide a summer heat

Yet in still time stands still for you as your internal beings continue to meet

You vs. you in a battle of winner take all while we wait for the results to see

Fight on champion, fight on little one, fight

Fight on for the day, fight for tomorrow fight for the night

There's no gentleness in this war and in the end someone must lose

The victor and the defeated only you must decide and chose.

Meaningful/ Meaningless

As I live within this world today, I find myself looking around at all the people and circumstances upon us and it leaves me in a state of confusion- concern. The question: "what means the most to me/ to us" is what wonders through my mind. Whatever the object of your affection may be, just how are you treating it and how do you make it fulfill its purpose. Think of this, if it is love, are you giving it freely, do you show it daily, say it, live it or do you let it go assumed and unheard. How about if it is money; do you use it to help others or just yourself? Perhaps you have it sitting up somewhere refusing to touch it? The scenarios could extend to include you and your life and just how are you living it. Regardless the object of the person, the fact will always be the same; if what means the most to you isn't being used in a meaningful manner it will always be meaningless.

Good Times

Damn! Damn! Damn James!

Yes all family matters but ease up on the growing pains

Around this bonanza we don't get to be familiar with Mr. Rogers and his neighborhood

You get the cabbage patch dolls while we just have the garbage pail kids and it ain't all good

It is indeed a different world for us than where you come from

Real life Evans, stuck in the heart of the ghetto until kingdom come

We hope to ease on down the road and do our Jefferson walk

But we still find ourselves sitting with Sanford and his son kicking that jive talk

Across the street there's Archie and all his family

Neither one of us live like the Cosby's yet he think he's better than me

In this jungle book, 21 jump street kills black males but that's just the facts of life

Pookie ran out of dope and tired of living so under the bridge is where he beats his crack wife

That's my momma calling me from the porch of 227, so you already know what's happening

The street lights are coming on and I'm not looking to have my butt whipped again

I know who's the boss and it definitely isn't me

She told me before that she's not giving any more breaks unless it's Doogie I need to see

It's hard to be living single so in precision like a team we must be

She's like the hulk with patience so like Webster with time is me

So I say peace to my buddy and let these Pro Wings begin to take flight

Too young to be a Knight rider because I have to be home before it gets night

Soul of the Stars

As I gaze into the space in which my name is being called
I listen to my life speak to me from a point of time being stalled
The stars have names but too many to being to mention
For fear of an absent mind of accomplishments for those sitting behind the partition
My loves that loved me more so they gave all they had so that I may get
I get the point of their loss for me to win so this life of mine is ready and set
Go with the wind and take to the stars as I begin to walk amongst giants
Towering and empowering my soul to strive for immeasurable empowerment
They look down on me as I look up to them
They sit watching and waiting for my next move as I begin to embody him
Him on whom I am to be and from this conception I was destined
Speak the truth the masses and seek deep with to see the life manifested
Force that they have imparted upon me so that I may light the flicker within the youth
No flame is to die, it must be taken for warmth, power and truth

The baptism of water isn't what was needed for the fire will purge us from our own sin
"Tell them", they said, "of the true power that we left within
We are sitting and watching every move that you all make
Tell them to not allow our sacrifice to have been a tragic mistake
We were indeed honored to have given our all so that you all may begin to bear witness
Freedom, justice and equality isn't free at all and what you know you must confess
Fear not a man for we shall always be with you
The power of 10,000 of 10,000 souls are here to support and protect you
Heralds of Angels and guardians we stand side by side fueling your soul
Fight on my children, fight until you have reached the necessary goal
Fight on my child, for the future of you and just know that with each breath
Never allow yourself to weary for to have true life, there must be death."

Dear white America,

I hope this letter finds you in the best frame of mind so that you are open to all that I am about to tell you. Let me first begin by saying that I must address you as white America because this is how you have dressed yourself. Please note that in order for me to address you in such fashion, you had to have first dressed yourself in that fashion (Hence the word address - adding dress to your dress). You have posed the questions; (1) why do we (black Americans/African-Americans call each other brothers and sisters, (2) why do we believe that laws and the playing field isn't on the same level for all Americans and (3) why don't we stop talking about slavery and the effects of it? Well hopefully, by the end of this letter you will understand and change your viewpoint on these matters. Let me also say that this isn't meant to be a pass on anyone's behalf but it is to serve as a wake up slap, so to speak, to help you all to stop saying dumb stuff such as "you people". With that being said, let us begin.

We refer to each other as brother and sister because we are indeed that. We are brothers and sisters in the struggle for freedom, justice and equality. We are siblings historically speaking, taking our roots back to our mother land and we are siblings in the fact that we, unlike you, are not the common enemy/violators of other ethnic groups/nationalities. We neither propelled ourselves as being the overseers of any other group nor invaded any other land and then deemed them as savages for standing up for themselves. We are indeed the global majority and the original inhabitant of the land yet we have always been the most overlooked. It's funny how you know deep within your very being that you have always needed us and perhaps this is why you hate us so much. This country that you have time and time again claimed as "your country", which in fact you stole, was built off of the blood, sweat, tears and ingenuity of my brothers and sisters.

I do realize that so far this isn't what you desire to hear but I think you should continue to read and perhaps obtain some insight into your problems. Secondly, let's pretend for a moment that you were watching two persons working out and training for an upcoming event. Both were given all of the necessary tools to achieve success in the event but one of them decides that they do not wish to work out harder than the other. So they took it upon them self to poison the other and create an environment that makes it almost impossible for the other to win. Thereby creating an environment for them to be lazy and achieve success much easier. The poison is fed to their opponent daily and over a period of time it has weakened them, yet it hasn't killed them as the cheater would have hoped for.

Their opponent continues to train and attempt to rebuild their health but due to the constant poisoning, they cannot do it properly. Until one day, the one being poisoned learns of this attempt on their life and they then begin to seek other alternatives for food but psychologically the damage has been done. The body can now only become as strong as the mind will allow it to develop and due to the generational damage, there is only so much that can be done at a time. It took years and generations to get to the weakened state and it will take even long to get out of it. So you see, you are the cheater in this instance yet you actually believe that you have done nothing wrong... this is what is inferred by the statement "white privilege". You have been in a certain position for so long that, now you feel as though you are supposed to be there and cannot understand what the problem is... You and your demented thinking are the problem.

Lastly, there's slavery and the prolonged effects of it upon not only the Black Americans/ African-Americans, but also you as well. If you do not believe that slavery was so bad and that Jim Crow laws weren't that bad, then how about we reverse the role for the next 10 years....in fact I couldn't see you all surviving the next 10 weeks of that same brutal treatment. When the great depression came about, it was only you all that couldn't deal with it and killed yourselves in large numbers. In fact, I'm willing to go as far as to say that you wouldn't make it 10 days in slavery and under Jim Crow laws. History has proven that your bodies can't tolerate much strain and many conditions that my brothers and sisters can and have. This is not to say that we were made for such abuse but that we are like the straight shot of alcohol and you are the watered down version. This isn't to serve as an insult but a reality check. Black can be watered down to white but in order for white to make it to black, black must be added in high doses. (Try it with crayons).

In conclusion, I ask each and every one of you to search within yourself to find the answer to these questions: Why do I fear everyone different from me and perhaps this is why I hate them? Also, do I hate them so much because I see the weaknesses within myself and if so how do I fix it all?

Here are a few suggestions that I sincerely believe will help to alleviate the problems facing America and you. (1) Stop thinking and acting as if you are better than everyone and everything because you are NOT. Treat everyone as an equal and or as you would like to be treated or better. No one is neither your servant nor subservient to you. (2) Relinquish what is rightfully NOT yours! In your possession are things that belong to just about everyone other than yourself, so hand it back over. (3) Stop meddling in everyone's affairs. Your doctrine/ dichotomy isn't the norm or the standard to which everything must be measured. In fact, to put it plainly for you to get- it's called RESPECT. (4) Stop living in "make believe" with Mr. Rogers and his neighborhood. Come back to reality and own up to the messes that you have caused and then pointed the finger at others. (5) Last but definitely not least, STOP KILLING US UNJUSTLY!!!!

If for some reason this seems as a task that is too hard for you to manage then just take the easy way out again…go kill yourself.

Cordially,

A Messenger

Pretend 'ish Talking

Talk that 'ish, just be sure you keep walking as you do
In fact, let me take just a moment to accompany you
Let's take a little stroll around this here dark corner
Now do me a little favor and repeat all that you said you goner
....No please don't get quite now, please say it all again
....Do you need a moment to recall or was it all just pretend
Well pretend you meant it and pretend like I didn't hear
Pretend you are as you pretended you are and not full or fear
Let's just pretend I fear you as you actually fear me
Let's just pretend for a moment that I'm as weak as you wished I would be
Let's just pretend I can't think and I really needed your complete guidance
And say for a moment that I enjoyed you standing over me in your squatting stance
Which I don't!
Now how about we pretend that I take you as amusing
And that the breath of life isn't what I foresee you stop using
How about we both pretend that your face wasn't introduced to the pavement
And that the amount of loss of blood didn't bring about much amusement

he he...
Wait did you call for help? Let's pretend I didn't hear that
I was too overwhelmed with thoughts of children dying that were black
You know they called for help to as never did they receive it
So I'll pretend as you once did therefore I won't quit
How many pint of blood does the human body really hold
Let's pretend the answer is only revealed once it's turned cold
Let's pretend that each pint represents a generation of mine that was lost
What? What was that you say? You're not ready to pay that type of cost
Well how about we pretend that I could care when in fact I couldn't careless
The one thing I'm currently concerned about is my shoes and who's going to clean up this mess
Oh well I guess it's the price you pay to rectify a wrong that's been done
This pretend may seem a bit over kill but I see it a battle in the war that's won.

The American Dream

The American dream
As fictitious as it may seem
Is a nightmarish of a dream
Black lives that matter and white that's doubtful
Hopeful of the promise that came as a lying mouthful
Shout full
Despiteful of the fact that Malcolm cried foul
So what can I do
I can take up the touch that others try to diminish
Replenish
Not finish
Just desiring to be all that I am to be
Possibly
Perhaps tell the tale of a young man growing into a man
Able to stand
A man that's not conformed to begging but demanding
Rightfully so it must be for me to be standing
These boots were made for walking
Quit talking
Stand up and take a stand against all that is but shouldn't be
He did, could I, should I, didn't he
Indeed
I shall proceed
Be all I can be is this the American dream

If so mist I not attempt to live as one free would deem
Bethune fresh air and living in a world where I am not subjected to the subjection of your torture
Neglected by all that is good and ridiculed with bad fortune
Shameful acts of animals placed on pedestals in over a black face
Treat us worse than the least yet follow our lineage down to the last trace
Misplaced aggression that's so egressions
Mislead us
Yet before us you were lost In the wilderness chasing your own tails
Lost in translation of stories misguiding and false tales
Let's recap this story line and reevaluate the dream that's missing
A nightmarish of a dream for us is giving and insisting
Insisting that we are mistaken and this dream is for all those that have the desire
Yes a dream of a sleeper for an awaken mind understands that you sir are a liar.

Conversation

Joe: "How is your son since I saw him last?"
Bill: "He's well. How is yours, might I ask?"
Joe: "He is doing better since we had a discussion that was much needed."
Bill: "Yea the birds and bees talk. So how did you proceed?"
Joe: "Actually I'm referring to police, society, the laws of this land and how they pertain to him."
Bill: "Oh that's good. He's such a good young man and not like them."
Joe: "Them who? To what them are you referring?"
Bill: "Those thugs I had to call the police on the other day with all that gang banging and cussing."
Joe: "What do you mean the other day??"
Bill: "Yea. Well it was a few at the corner acting a fool but this one in particular that came walking my way."
Joe: "Did he threaten you or try to harm you? What did you do or say?"
Bill: "No, not directly I suppose. I saw him from a distance walking down my street."
Joe: "So was he harassing someone else or whom else did he meet?"
Bill: "Well after I called the police to alert them of a suspicious character carrying a gun and walking my way."
Joe: "Wait! Are you for certain what was in his hand? A

gun did you say?"

Bill: "I believe it was. Whatever these thugs carry now a days?"

Joe: "How certain of this are you and what happened when the police arrived?"

Bill: "I couldn't wait forever for them so I fired a few shots at him to stand my ground."

Joe: "You did what?! Did you hit him? Did he fall to the ground?"

Bill: "No. Unfortunately I missed; I think it's only because I've never used it before."

Joe: "What do you mean unfortunately? And you shot at him from inside your door?"

Bill: "Yea, ha-ha, and the bastard ran away before I could reload and try again."

Joe: "Try again? Why didn't you ascertain as to whom he was and if he was just visiting a friend?"

Bill: "No need to take unnecessary chances these days because that punk could have harmed me or my family."

Joe: "Bill you neither know not what you are saying nor what you did or didn't see."

Bill: "You must be kidding? You have no idea what I saw and what I saw was a potential threat."

Joe: "You saw what you wanted to and with saw it with your heart full of hate."

Bill: "Hate? I'm a Christian I can't hate anyone."

Joe: "Hate indeed you possess and showed it with pointing

of your gun."

Bill: "You're just a liar! How dare you question me and what I know to be true?"

Joe: "Bill you are a liar and the truth isn't in you."

Bill: "Joe I can't believe what I'm hearing...I thought you were one of the good ones and not like those thugs saying only black lives matter."

Joe: "Thugs?! You label them as thugs because they believe that we shouldn't be abused, killed, mistreated or targeted as if we didn't matter."

Bill: "Not actually... it's because…"

Joe: "Because we have chosen to stand up for ourselves and we have a just cause."

Bill: "No, what I'm saying is…"

Joe: "Is that you have purposely chosen to not face reality and actually is."

Bill: "You're being just another abrasive, loud and threatening nig..."

Joe: "What did you just call me? Fix your mouth before I fox your wig!"

Bill: "This is what I mean. This is why we must arm ourselves against such barbarians like you."

Joe: "Barbarians? You must have me confused with those of lesser hue."

Bill: "No you and those thugs saying that only black lives matter."

Joe: "The only problem is that you and those like you don't

believe that they matter at all. In fact you only think that you matter."
Bill: "Why can't you just stop with the disruptive behavior and stay in your place."
Joe: "That's it! Let me break something down to you for once and for all before I smash your face!"
Bill: "This is what I mean...so angry. So hostile. Why must..."
Joe: "Why must I what? Defend myself against oppressors like you that abuse others trust."
Bill: "What I was about to say was..."
Joe: "Perhaps you're the real victim and I'm the victimizor without a real cause..."
Bill: "Exactly my point..."
Joe: "Down your nose and your gun are the only things you point."
Bill: "You people get on my nerves with your backwards thinking. Either it's be the victim or be the only victim; either way you're just being too lazy to get up and take advantage of all the opportunities that we have given you."
Joe: "You gave who? You gave yourself? Who exactly did 'you' give it to?"
Bill:" All you negr.... colo...black folks." My great-great-granddaddy fought for your freedom and this is the thanks we get. Just be grateful and shut up!"
Joe: "I'll be grateful when you stop seeing me and mine as slaves on the plantation. I'll be grateful when we no longer

have to protest and fight for equality. I'll be grateful when overseers stop murdering and unjustly locking us up."
Bill: "What the fu..."
Joe: "I'll fact. I'll be grateful when you sons of bitches stop profiling and shooting at my son when all he wanted to do was return the book that he borrowed from YOUR son the other day."
Bill: "Excuse me? What did you just say?"
Joe: "You heard me right! That was my son that you shot at and called the police on the other day. That's why I know that you're just another racist and sorry excuse for a human being."
Bill: "Oh I didn't..."
Joe: "You didn't know? That's because you never took the time to. That's ok because I didn't..."
Bill: "What didn't you do?"
Joe: "I didn't call the police because I'm going to beat you until you're black and blue."

What Do You See

If a picture is worth a thousand words

Then anything less than 100 million for my life would be absurd

Through the marching on of time we learn to deal

We begin to view the world for what is truly real

Although some wish to continue to dwell in Never Never land

Six out of ten of us allow out mind to expand

Friends, Romans, countrymen lend me your ear

Listen to the divine rather than be overcome with fear

Sometimes in life you have to just roll the dice and see what will happen

Be that early bird rather than get caught cat napping

Open your eyes, don't keep them shut to what's actually going on

Tell Rodney King "Hell no, we can't all just get along!"

Why should we, when in fact everyone knows we are not the same

Some have, while others only dream of fortune and fame

So now my question is, to be or not to be

That really all depends on what is it you wish to see.

Silence

How many tears must I cry before I am eased with what I must do?

Allah why is my heart so sorrowful at my attempt to please you?

My heart aches, my soul is weary and my nerves feel shot

However I know that this small sacrifice I must accomplish in order to keep me from burning hot

Not just in the next life but in this one as well

Heaven is my focal point not the burning pits of hell

Out of the 7 levels you have created, I want to be at the top

Therefore, in check I must be and conversation I must stop

I desire my blessing so greatly that this small thing I know I can do

Not for my sake nor anyone else but solely for the sake of you

You are Ar-Rasheed so I know I shall be rightly guided

From this I seek your pleasure and more consciously minded

Allah please forgive my sins and ease me of my distress

I know from your mercy I shall not cause a complete mess.

Final Goal

Today I met my destiny

It started directly thru the soul of me

I never could have imagined the immense heat it would infuse within

An enormous amount of radiant energy combustion soon began

Kaboom! With no reservation it soon sounded

Kaboom! Negation of hesitation in unison we compounded

1+1=2 yet these 2 became 1

How can this be so when I was with none?

So shall it be in end as it was so in the beginning

So this beginning begot this, what was once thought to be the ending

Yet there is an end, and end to what once was

A never ending story of living yet dying from unrequited love

No need for tears in this story for it has a process that continues to proceed

Pro-seed indeed come forth with blossoms aside of fragrance and please hold the weeds

Say it again, say it for me and say it slow as not to combine

Wait just one minute could this mirage actually be so

Why yes indeed for as so above so is below

Victory is finally here and upon me I can feel the warmth permeating every faced of my soul

Who would have ever thought that loving and knowing oneself would make peace the final goal?

Individual

To be an individual is to be free

Free to express my own unique individuality

Freedom to choose which path that I wish to call my own

Respect for self as well as my family home

To stand proud and firm on my personal beliefs, values and thoughts

To know that my ideas and personality was never bought

To stand proud and speak out loud "I am my own man!"

To never ever leave my life in someone's else's hand

To know that I was born with my own creative mind

To not live my life led by the hand as if I was blind

To go and come as I so choose

To be successful and not think that I was born just to lose

I am a man regardless of what you may think of me

I must be steadfast in what I know to be right and wrong

I do not need to be told what to think as a child but like a grown individual I think on my own

I urge all of my brothers and sisters to be bold and proud

Stand up, sat that you're an individual and be sure to say it loud!

Racing Race

Money talks and bullshit walks so with that, why are you still here
You've lied about far too much for way too long; so it's best if we part right here
Enough is enough and enough of your misleading and deceiving I've reached
You've erased my history, misguided my youth, there's so much to be un-teached
Untaught, untrained, unconditioned and un-blinded
Erased our past, stolen our future so presently our minds are too confounded
It's time to free their dome, you have kept them free and dumb for far too long
Freedom isn't free but it truly free when you're not living completely wrong
Misguided youth believing what a deceitful society has fed to their youthful mind
Leading them to the path of destruction and not seeing the beauty if their own kind
Freedom, justice and equality is the natural evolution of man's desire
Slavery, death and destruction is how you hung us on the wire
Lynched by suppressed ambitions and thoughts that roamed free into space

Lynched by ill begotten direction from the misconception that you don't hate my face
Running in this race of racism with racists that have chained me to the starting block
So the competition can stroll along the course while we grow weary fighting other stock
Marketing us on the auction the time it will take to eventually give in
Even if we manage to break these chains, you poisoned the team so now how shall we still win
It is what it is and it ain't what it ain't
I'd rather die trying to be triumphant than to give up in a faint
Regardless of the number of us that you manage to turn against the collective
Collectively we still shall persevere until we reach our objective
Freedom, justice and equality is as it has always been
The dream of those gone past for the reality of the future to be seen
Break these shackles on our feet and hands, loosen the hypnosis on our minds
Restructure the course to be ran and steady those blurred lines
Our vision is clear and the path is yet laid forth
Once this concept becomes a reality we can see just what you're worth.

Souls of Black Folks

The souls of black folks tremble at the thought of what is to come
The majority lay under the minority while the minority keep the majority under their thumb
Which is which when the reversal is how society seems to give off the picture
Notwithstanding the deferred hopes and dream's dismal capture
Pray for forgiveness while they pray for salvation
Looking to bring back days of old while the old stay deluded by reparation
Strive for doing for self and not still watching time walking by and by
Focus your vision of the road ahead instead of the pie in the sky
The souls of black folks breath the air of life into the liberty that must come
Justice avoiding just us, no freedom for the free and dumb
It's not free you know while the dome is still shackled in chains
Chained to memory of a notion that fell ill in infested brains
It's the black plague that was spoke of and still it exist
Killing a new generation of souls that old souls hoped it would miss

Yet it did not and it could not, especially when it was embedded with the blood line
A ticking time bomb of destruction that continues to divide me and mine
Perhaps tomorrow will come and the cure will be accepted
Yet it was given before and then too it was rejected.

Justice or Else

Why can't we have something of our own without you being involved?
Are there some issues that should be discussed that haven't been resolved?
Why must you take offense when we decide to unite without your participation or feeling neglected?
Is it that you realize that once we unite firmly that our power and presence will be respected?
Why must you feel so threatened by our essence that you would kill us unarmed, naked and without cause?
Does our sexual prowess intimidate you so much that concern for wellbeing doesn't give you much pause?
Is your conscious picking at you for the misdeeds that you have committed?
Whom is it that you are seeking to take this country back since you first stole it?
Perhaps you need help checking off the list, so assistance I shall give
The Natives you first deceived, poisoned and ceased them to live
Africans you kidnapped, murdered and enslaved
Oh and plus you disallowed them to obtain legal assistance and when it was sought YOU became enraged
The Latinos you abused, used and then after, threw them in the mix with the African
The Asians you imprisoned and ridiculed as much as you

possibly can
All of which you invaded and demolished their lands
depleting of resources above and below the surface
Are these the ones in which you feel are attempting to take
your precious place?
Which of these are you referring to when you say you want
to take "your" country back from?
Should I also mention the question of back to where and
where from?
We gave ourselves the UNIA, NOI, Black Panthers and
now Black Lives Matter
You cried victim and screamed murder as the ceiling began
to shatter
We said no justice, no peace and equal rights and
empowerment for all
You poisoned the cause and set the leaders up for a full
blown media fall
Each time a head rises up you quickly send your minions to
knock it back down
A complete 3 ring circus and only the audience can tell
who's the clown
Someone must be the ring master and someone has to play
the fool
Except this time around let's change up the role of who's
the tool
Our time is coming for each generation grows more and
more impatient than the previous

The marchers have marched on; it's justice or else and we mean it.

Blind Men

Blind men being lead to the gallows where many men have gone to never return
Marching to the drum of blood falling to the ground as a cistern
Drip...drip...drip...goes the blood as it falls to the earth
Counting down the seconds until the sickle of death has taken all that they are worth
No more than a memory etched into the psyche of children singing ring around the rosy
Blind men wandering in the wilderness of this barren land that's feeds on their souls
Wolves tracking the spilled blood that still fill discarded bowls
Drip...drip...drip onto the ground to give life to the roots that lie beneath
Roots being fed the life that the past once bequeath
Sprouting forth as them dry bones reach for the sky
The marrow within the core drips forth as each bone becomes dry
Life source depleting, bones being weakened and soon overcome with aching
Drip...drip...drip onto the ground spills the last remaining chances for existence
Limbs not producing fruit because roots are dying off due to lack of persistence

Blind man why can't you see that if you just open your eyes you wouldn't be led astray
the path is just before you if you would only go the other way.

Consciously Stupid

I think it's time to resurrect the original Black Panther Party
It's time to be a power force for our community and not still mentally tardy
Socially unequipped, economically inadequate and unjustly unjustifiably tortured for daily existence
Persistence
Is needed and most importantly the empowerment of the people
Black on black disrespect of youth and old
Girl against woman, man against boy is how the game is sold
Passing the baton in the race for slavery, who can beat who to the trap
Caught like mice searching for the biggest piece of cheese when you can't read the map
F- U B, with a laugh and wondering what's so funny
Don't you see yourself in the face that you cursed out dummy
So stupidly blind to the fact that each tree has roots and grows depending on the cotter
If the fruit is bad then check the poison in the Flint water
You are accepting the virus while rejecting the cure and yet you hate that which is best
Looking favorably upon the killer and wishing the killed would just give it a rest

So rest in pieces of memories of being fed in the morning and being protected at night
The soldiers of yesterday are mostly gone, the rest are too old to fight
The new breed of today are disappointing and too confused
They spend too much time arguing not realizing they're all being used
J Edger would be proud of the work that he has done
He picked up where Willie left off leaving the score 300 to none
They enslaved the mind then the enslaved it some more
The body was far too easy, now the slave is a happy whore
At first it was a process to break the will and spirit of our blood line
Then it became a testimony of the genius plan to us against our kind
Now it is simply a repeat of the washing and rewashing of the brain
Simply put, hands off policy for the consciously stupid you don't need to train.

Beaten Heart

Domestic violence is real
Hearts being beaten with no physical feel
Emotions running wild with fire that burns the soul
Burning desire uncontrolled and lost without a goal
Lacking direction
Unattainable perfection
Broken mirrored images that distort reality
Fumbling blind fury fighting with eyes that can't see
Swinging in every direction not hitting anything that should be hit
Innocent bystanders becoming victims then later a misfit
Misfire, mismatched, misconstrued, mistreated
Missourian minded, misapplied misbehavior that mishaps mistreated
Take one for the Gipper
Gilligan or the Skipper
Which ever direction the storm has taken you
Just remember to thy own self be true
Beat down, beat up, beaten into what seems like nothing at all
Heart broken, mildly stroken' by rocks down the cliff to fall
The apocalypse has turned into the solar eclipse that hangs over my day
Blinding my horizon of sunshine and darkening the better

way
Better days have come and gone and perhaps one day they shall come again
With every beat upon me I take is a beat my heart stopped and tries to begin again.

MLK

One shot, two shots, three shots, four
Cops killing blacks, whites killing more
We holds these truth to be self-evident
No matter the time, blacks are still seen as irrelevant
From Africa to America, from America back to Africa under Apartheid
Regardless the form of racism, a part I died
Segregation and verbal desegregation to tribulation with capitulation
Integration linked to sex without mutual climaxes with a stipulation
As long as I owe you, you'll never be broke...
Ergo, you can't get nothing, so just accept being broke
Broken, taken, used and cast to the waist side
Graves expanding street corners and city blocks wide
Ferguson, Baltimore, Chicago and Flint were all just the witnesses of the whole thing
Each voice that rises is another Martyr Lose a King
Marcus taught the leaders something that many seem to have skipped that class
Get your own fair share, basically just get up off your ass
Beggars can't be choosers, so why not chose to stop begging for scrap
Especially when within our very own we have so much potential left to tap.

Heaven and Hell

They want to carry guns but don't want to enlist
It's like the wild, wild west yet they do not want us to have any bullets
They got guns
We can't have any
They can carry openly
We can't have any
They taking over land
We can't have any
They have wealth
We can't have any
They have welfare
We can't have any
They have jobs
We can't have any
They have education
We can't have any
They get police protection
We can't have any
They have the right to speak out
We can't have any
They have all rights to do as they please
We can't have any.....
So let me ask you this; what the hell can we have?
Besides the bullets from your guns

We help to build your wealth
We get blamed for your welfare
We watch you become educated
We have the right to remain silent before, during and after receiving ass whippings from police
We only have the right to be seen and never heard as children do
Not do anything that may infringe upon you and your right to take our lands
Not protest as you treat our men, women and children as moving prey
So the question I must really ask; why the heaven you get and the hell must I have?

Double Talk

I find it quite strange…
How we can have different meanings while saying the same thing?
I pledge allegiance to the flag of the divided states of America
And to the racism in which it stands
Two nations, under God
Completely denying true liberty and justice for all.

Fred Hampton

One day my child, I will not be coming home
Each day has been a struggle that has been greater than my own
My struggle for freedom is necessary in order for you to exist
My struggle for equality must become more than just another urban myth
My struggle for justice is real and must not be denied to just us
Give me liberty or give me death, so if it is so than it is a must
Oppression is worse than slaughter so they slaughter us because we're tired of being oppressed
Countless names have become martyrs, so in death they become blessed
Blessed to be removed from this necessary unnecessary struggle just to be able to live at peace
So now it is necessary to necessarily keep and maintain my piece
My beloved brother once told us that he was a Revolutionary
As the new day has come the time remains the same that I too must stand with posterity
I Am a Revolutionary; so I AM definitively just as I Am suppose

Contrary to what the opposition would like to believe, I will not be in repose
I Am as I must for in the end I will be as I should be
I Am a living Revolutionary, for the I Am is in me.

Pawn Stars

Would someone please elaborate on the personality and characteristics of We the people
For when I look around me I don't see myself in that group
I see it referring to a group that has land, are rich, white and male
I see they constituted a more perfect union for them and them alone
Sure there are those that believe that they are included
But they are not
They think that just because they have some money and land that their black faces will be over looked
But it will not
Then there are those that think that they can buy and kiss enough butt to get in the crowd
But they will not
Some think that that they can sell enough butt to get their way in
But they cannot
Some even have the same complexion as those that so called founded a stolen land believe they get a pass
But they will not
Same skin tone except you don't have the right features, NO MA'AM
So you will not
Yes you produce more of them for them but don't get it

misunderstood, that's your only purpose
Again, no you will not
Then there are those that say, "I may not have land or money but I look exactly like you my brother"
But you too will not
"I fight your causes for you and I go where you say go"
Again, you too will not
In the end, We the people are just that; We the only people that matter
We the rich, white males of the world established a more perfect union amongst ourselves for the sole purpose of the betterment of ourselves
In the end everyone else are just pawns that we move as we see fit.
Check.

Word Usage

How often is it that we think of the words we use and what it is they actually mean as well as how they may influence the mentality of not only ourselves but also the individual to whom we are directing them towards? How many times in a day do you use the following words: kid, nigger/ nigga, bitch, dog, or even friend? What do these words (among countless others) denote as oppose to the context in which they are used? Let's begin with the most common which is kid; which when used is referring to a child/ young person. However, it is actually the term used to describe a young goat. Although it has more than one meaning its first and original meaning is a young goat- not a young child. So why is it that we have become so accustomed to depicting our children as greedy animals yet we get upset when they begin to conduct themselves as animals… why is this? Secondly, we have a term that has and is still defined as an offensive slang term, in fact the first definition say that is used as a disparaging (belittle/ degrading) term for a black/ dark skinned person. Nevertheless, we (being the lost people we are) have transformed this murderous word into something that's supposed to be cool and vastly acceptable but only when used by those of like complexion. Only a few decades back it was viewed as an insult and refuted by all those of the dark complexion…What happened to us?

Then we come to two words that are closely related yet with different levels of acceptability- dog and the infamous bitch. Now if a dog refers to an animal and bitch is the female counterpart of the male dog, why do we transform these words into male and female (human) titles? Is it because we either think of or view/ want our women as lewd, spiteful or overbearing. Maybe it's because we feel that by downplaying them we can somehow over-play ourselves. This isn't possible nor probable due to the fact that a nation (people) cannot rise any higher than the women in it. So as long as we continue to beat down our women we are continually sealing our fate with destruction. With that being said there's no need to expound upon the usage of dog and how it affects the mentality of males, especially young Afro-American males (not black because that is a color and not an ethnicity).

In fact one of my teachers, Imam W.D. Muhammad, taught us that most English words can be broken up to find the meaning behind it (by removing the first letter of the word). For example, take the word "black". We have come to know this word as previously stated, however if you remove the first letter of the word, you will see B-lack. This is to say that all those that are labeled as such (by whites) are lacking "B". By laying this letter on its side, it takes on the characteristic of the Phoenician letter for bull as well as male testicles. There are numerous of other words within the English language that this applies to as well, and I suggest you take a moment to research a few; such as sword (i.e. s-word/ secret word/ scared word).

Last but not least is the misplaced and misunderstood meaning and usage of friend and to whom it should be placed upon. Everyone cannot be friends nor could you be viewed as everyone's friend. To be a friend one must like, trust, support or sympathize with not just the one you are familiar with seeing. You could be someone's friend but not have them as yours so it is of the utmost importance that we be extremely careful as to whom we think of as being "our" friend; because sometimes what we think is mutual could in fact be only our perception and not a shared reality.

There are numerous words that we tend to inappropriately use such as can and may (can demotes ability while may is for permission), could and would (could is for ability and would is for a desire or request), farther and further (farther as in the root word far is for physical distance while further is the metaphorical or figurative); however since there are so many misrepresented words I ask that we begin to think of the words we use and just what they actually mean. Words that have the ability to heal or to harm, it all depends on which word, when and how we use it. As it states in the Bible "…life and death are in the power of the tongue…" and also in the belief of Islam, when it was asked of Prophet Muhammad (peace be upon him) what was the best part of the body he said the tongue and when asked about the worst part he also said the tongue. So be careful as to what you say and what you accept.

Thoughts on America

Now what I'm about to say should not be taken the wrong way but just imagine what the outcome would be- Since the election of the President Obama and now the Trayvon situation, America has been revealing its true colors more and more. It has been showing the amount of hatred, racism, ethnocentric, and just plain foolishness that has been not overlooked but understated since the civil rights movement. If America doesn't begin to take a firm and humanly stand on these detrimental issues very soon it will find itself without the option of actual justice but more of a vigilante justice, which in turn will send this country into a spiral of catastrophic deterioration. What if all of the killings and hate crimes began to be reversed, meaning that for every one incident of a Caucasian killing an African American, two Caucasians were killed by African Americans?? How involved would the judicial system become and how quickly would they do it? It has been over 40 days since Trayvon was slain; his murderer is identified yet no formal charges have been filed??? Where in the History of these United States has a President ever been as disrespected as our current one? This country is on the verge of exploding, it will be the exploding of the American dream...Thanks for the heads up Langston Hughes for telling us what happens to a Dream Deferred.

Complaining About A Complaint

Republicans, Democrats, Liberals Oh My
Tea party, green party, Vote or Die
We wanted to talk about issues so they talk about it
The issues were talked about, so now what?
Talk about them some more
So they talked about them some more
50 years later they still talked about them
100 years later they talked about them some more
Point of order.....when will the talking stop and the action begin?
That depends on when will you stop only asking for them to talk about the issues
Stop talking and start implementing
At which point the issue will then be; why are you asking for more than what's been given to you?
You wanted jobs after we freed you from slavery, so we gave you share cropping
Then you complained about the pay
You wanted your own after slavery, so we gave you Segregation
Then you complained about inequality of it
You didn't like being three fifth of a citizen, so we gave you civil rights
Then you complained about us respecting it

You wanted to have the right to buy a house wherever you want
Then you complained about the price and interest hike
You complained about public policy and thought a black president would make it better
Then you complained when you got one and we disrespected him just like you
After all this time has passed and all of your complaining, do you really think a quick protest will force us to do anything more than has been done???
Or must we hear another complaint about that as well?
How about you start complaining about what you are not doing for yourself.
We will take care of ourselves so you should start taking care of yourselves.

The Sisters

The emperor has no clothes Lady Liberty
Don't you see the child that you bore never loved me
Your sister is blindfolded yet peeking from under her mask
She has the sword in one hand and scales that don't way to task Equally measured so equally yoked
This side against that side and yet it is my life that continues to be choked
Smothered, killed, mutilated and maimed
Sick and tired of playing the Ring Around the Rosie game
White America hates Black America, Asians, Latinos and others
White, rich men is White America the rest are just the bastard cousins
Misused and discarded as slop for the pigs to feast upon
Lady, could you please tell me the logic in giving thanks for being cut out like cheap a coupon
Gentle souls slaughtered for no more than the opportunity to do so
Lady if you're not sure, perhaps your sister would know
As you sit on high viewing the injustice taking place, your sister stands idly by bearing witness
Must we all begin to flip the flag to signal distress?
We didn't cause this construct so why are we to blame that it is resolved
Blind woman, if you don't being to fix it, when the sword is

snatched don't you dare become appalled
You can keep those scales since they seem to be broken anyway
Resolved to revolt against all that stands in the way our true independence day
Power to the people of this oppressing land that no longer can stand the oppression
Justice will be seen, freedom will be felt and equality will not be an omission.

www.ingramcontent.com/pod-product-compliance
Lightning Source LLC
Chambersburg PA
CBHW071408040426
42444CB00009B/2147